Through My Eyes

poems by

Melissa Grossman

Finishing Line Press
Georgetown, Kentucky

Through My Eyes

Copyright © 2017 by Melissa Grossman
ISBN 978-1-63534-218-5 First Edition
All rights reserved under International and Pan-American Copyright Conventions.
No part of this book may be reproduced in any manner whatsoever without written permission from the publisher, except in the case of brief quotations embodied in critical articles and reviews.

ACKNOWLEDGMENTS

The following poems were previously published:

Driving Home — *Kansas City Voices*
My 8th Birthday — *Quintessence*, Ventura Country Writers' 2008 Anthology
Room With a View — *Windows*, Ventura Country Writers' 2010 Anthology
This Girl — *Common Ground*
Vanishing Point — *Solo Novo*
Wee Body — *Common Ground*
While Baubie Sleeps — *In the Company of Women: An Anthology of Wit & Wisdom, Sass & Class*

Publisher: Leah Maines

Editor: Christen Kincaid

Cover Art: Melissa Grossman

Author Photo: Rosemary Grossman

Cover Design: Elizabeth Maines McCleavy

Printed in the USA on acid-free paper.
Order online: www.finishinglinepress.com
 also available on amazon.com

> Author inquiries and mail orders:
> Finishing Line Press
> P. O. Box 1626
> Georgetown, Kentucky 40324
> U. S. A.

Table of Contents

Wee Body 1
In the Pool with Mother 2
Child's Play 3
Father & Daughter Time 4
My 8th Birthday 5
Fat Girl 6
You Think I Don't See You 7
My Father's Slippers 8
This Girl 9
Desire 10
Room with A View 11
While Baubie Sleeps 12
Hair on Fire 13
Driving Home 14
Passover 1985 15
At the Supermarket 16
The Day Our Dad Died 17
The Necklace 18
When I Was Little 19
Real Estate 20
Immersion 21
Saying Goodbye 22
Dusk 23
After 24
Vanishing Point 25

WEE BODY

Wee body
takes to water
a guppy,
rubbery
limbs awriggle.
In cool blue,
she floats
free—flying
in liquid sky.
Her squidgy skin
atingle, her
fingers dimple
with wrinkles.
Her shadow
ripples below,
loose
from her.

IN THE POOL WITH MOTHER

Weightless, we three
cling to her like barnacles,
as she bounces in the water,
our podgy bodies bobbing up and down,
hold tight to our mother ship,
waves flowing from our vortex.
At our insistence, she sings
> *The king is in his altogether, but altogether, his altogether,*
> *he's altogether as naked as the day that he was born…*
And then…
she dunks herself underwater,
taking us with her.
And we all come up together,
completely wet with glee.

CHILD'S PLAY

At the park I like to swing
on the monkey bars,
let my feet dangle
and sway. A bigger kid
helps me reach the high bar.
My arms feel strong, like
they could hold on forever.
Last night I saw the crescent moon
smiling in the sky.
I reached it without any help,
and swung on it till morning.

FATHER & DAUGHTER TIME

Every night in bed at an early hour,
my father always wore a thick terry cloth robe
beneath a heated blanket.
As a girl, I'd climb onto the king-size bed
and nestle snugly under his left arm.
We watched television together,
though I don't remember what—maybe
Slattery's People or *Perry Mason*—I'm not sure.
I only remember
how my head used to rise and fall
on his chest with each breath,
and how I tried to breathe along with him,
breath for breath, and how
I'd press my ear to his chest
and fall asleep listening to his heart:
lub-dub, lub-dub, lub-dub…

MY 8TH BIRTHDAY
    after Frank O'Hara

I had my 8th birthday in Hawaii
where my brothers and I spent
our whole vacation on the beach
(except on Wednesdays and Sundays)
when we watched them bury the pig
to bake for the big luau, only we didn't
go to the luau, because we didn't
like poi so when my parents asked me
what I wanted to do for my birthday,
I said I wanted to see "HELP!"
because it was my favorite movie
and I loved the Beatles, especially George,
though "HELP!" was really about Ringo,
and how one of his rings was meant
for the Great Kahili, which of course I knew
because I'd already seen it four times before
and afterwards we went to Chef's Coffee Shop for dinner,
where I told the waitress that I wanted "the usual"
and they knew to make me a
sandwich—grilled cheese.

FAT GIRL

I carry the weight of being a fat girl.
I bear the indelible sledgehammer taunts:
    my brothers call me "tank"
        people say "how beautiful" I'd be if I "just lost weight."
I wear the weight like battle armor.

I carry the raw egg of my future on a spoon.

YOU THINK I DON'T SEE YOU

You think I don't see you,
don't notice your absence
in the dance hall. I see you
outside in the cold, night air.
Your back facing the hall.
You try to unfeel your loneliness,
to pretend you aren't hurt
no one has asked you dance.
The handful of you out there
only makes you feel worse,
a reject among rejects.
You think, if only you weren't
a sweet overlooked turnip,
things would be different.
You wish you were me,
so you would be here—inside,
moving.

MY FATHER'S SLIPPERS

Awakened from sleep, I hear
the shuffle of my father's slippers
against the ceramic tile. My dog,
snuggled beside me, hears them too.
He leaps out of bed, his dog tags jangling;
follows my father down the hallway
to the kitchen. They have this time
alone together in the dark hours of morning,
every morning—a shared hunger
for something sweet. I dream
of catching my father
as he falls in the hallway.
Awakened again, I hear
the scuff of my father's slippers
on the hallway tile, walking back
to his bedroom; and my dog skipping behind him,
returns to my bed, his dog tags jangling.

THIS GIRL

She carried a dead coyote to class,
this girl who kept to herself.
Roadkill in her car, she drove to school,
this girl, with thick, unkempt hair.
When she told the professor
of her desire to draw the dead animal,
he polled the other students.
The drawing class gathered
in the courtyard, seated
around the dead coyote,
sketch pads tilted, raspy sound
of charcoal on paper.
This was her moment, this girl
sitting nearest the corpse, to capture
the lifeless limbs, the dangling tongue,
the matted fur, the gray pallor.
Soon, the stench of decay
drove all away. She was
the last to leave, this girl,
who, this one day,
came alive.

DESIRE

The suspense of your next kiss…my cheek
against your face…my head nestling…breathing in
…your flustered face, unbuttoning my blouse…
the newness… the tracing…your caress
…your weight pressing…my body rising…
your smile, watching…the blush
…the suspense of your next kiss…

ROOM WITH A VIEW
after Su Tung P'o

I don't know whether it is day or night.
Yet, soft light filters like lace through the low clouds.
I watch a lone swan preen its white wings.
A feather drifts winsomely past my window.
It appears luminous in the ethereal light,
where I am lost without you

WHILE BAUBIE SLEEPS
for Sarah Fruchtnis Pauker (1880-1980)

Yesterday I found drawings I made of my grandmother,
my *baubie*—as she slept, six months before she died.
It was the first time I had ever seen her still.
I used to plead with her to sit and visit.
She was always fussing, handing out *chatchkes*
from her gift stash, or serving hot tea.
Not wanting to wake her, I took pencil to paper.
As I drew I listened to her breathing,
thought of her crossing the Atlantic
with her baby, my Aunt Clara in her arms.
Later widowed, with three young children,
she worked as a peddler
selling house-dresses door-to-door;
my mother helping her carry her wares.
I remember the torn toilet paper squares
she prepared every week before Friday Shabbos,
because strict Jewish law forbids
any kind of work on the Sabbath.
She once stayed up past midnight emptying
one-serving sugar packets into a jar.
Often I sat with her while she ate dinner in her room—
the same dinner every night: boiled chicken,
baked potato, steamed carrots. Sitting on the side
of her bed, the tray in front of her,
she would carefully skin and bone the chicken leg,
cut it into bite-size pieces, then peel the skin
off the potato, and mash it into the carrots.
When she awoke, I showed her my drawing
and I remember how the corner of her mouth lifted
like a gentle slice of pink melon.

HAIR ON FIRE

My hair caught on fire. At a funeral. Actually, it was more like a memorial or a wake. The gathering took place in a rec. room… well, it was more like a community room, or a really nice living room that you had to reserve for special occasions. It was there that my hair caught on fire, fizzled like a hot fuse when I backed into a candle. The children of the deceased hosted a buffet luncheon (it was really a potluck, and everyone who came brought something). A lot of people came; it seemed like a hundred or so, but there were really 40 or 50 people, max. Everyone there stood up to share stories about the woman who had died…well, not everyone, but all the children did, and several close friends. I was so moved by one young girl who had spoken, I had to talk to her. She was in her teens, though I'm no judge of age, so she could have been younger. The girl told how the woman who had passed away treated her like a daughter, gave her confidence. She reminded me of how some people talked about my mother at her wake, wishing she were theirs. Laurie told me how she saw my mother as her role model when she raised her children. Or, maybe it was Sharon who said that. I don't remember. Then Iris pulled me aside, and then Irene, and then someone else and then another. The whole day is a blur. But the girl in the rec. room—I remember her—because she had long dark hair, like I have. Thinking of her, I thought of my mother, who was always kind to strangers, but insisted—in no uncertain terms—she hated my long hair. Ever since I was a little girl. It was because of her my hair caught fire.

DRIVING HOME

She haunts me, this young woman I drove home one evening.
Wan with hollow cheeks and mussed blond hair that fell over her face,
she kept me captive in my car, told stories about the room
she rented in a big house where no one talked to her.
She stared at a box of Girl Scout cookies on the floor by her feet,
so I gave her one. Watched her from the corner of my eye,
hold it to her mouth with both hands, like a mouse.
When we arrived at the house where she lived, I waited for her
to open the car door, but she kept talking and talking and talking -
wanting something from me I was afraid to give.
A half-hour later, she finally opened the door, then
turned back to look at me, and said *thank you.*
As she stepped out, I grasped the steering wheel, relieved
to drive away. A startling knock on the window made me stop.
She was still there, bending down to say *thank you* again,
but I knew she was really saying, *please.*

PASSOVER 1985

I set the table: the *seder* plate, *haggadahs*, wine, *matzoh*,
and the cup of Elijah, the immortal prophet.
The front door is opened to welcome him.
Aromas emanate from the kitchen:
chicken soup, simmering, noodle *kugel*, brisket.
Tables and chairs are needed from storage.
I open the closet door
and turn on the light, push aside
the clothes wrapped in cellophane, hanging overhead.
There I find my father's army uniform.
Dead just three months.
My father, the decorated battalion surgeon.
I yank the coat from the hanger,
hold it close, and sob.
Caught unprepared by the opened door.

AT THE SUPERMARKET

Screams sting the air,
heads pop and turn like small prey on alert.
The wild one holds the market captive.
So fierce, he will not be tamed, stands upright
in the cart, shakes his cage.
At checkout, as his mother empties her basket
the child hits her, bares his teeth, and roars.
Leaving the store, I can still hear him pitching.
I sit in my truck, wonder about the mother I might have been,
remember how trapped I felt as a little girl,
having to behave like a trained circus animal.
Suddenly I grab the steering wheel and scream,
and scream, and scream…
Outside my window in the parking lot,
I see the mother and her son return to her car,
and imagine she must be curious about the rocking truck,
and the raging woman inside.

THE DAY OUR DAD DIED

I can still hear them
after so many years.
I can still hear them in the backyard
outside my shuttered bedroom window.
I can hear them over my own sobbing,
remember how I imagined them embracing.
My twin brothers, thinking
themselves alone, together
untied their grief.
I can still hear them,
two grown men wailing,
utterly undone.

THE NECKLACE

It was bound to happen
after so many years,
the silk thread worn thin.
A garland of irreplaceable gems,
each unique, luminous.
Still, it came as a surprise
when it broke. One by one
each fell, and rolled
away, beyond my reach.
I collected what I could.
Spaces   now grace   the reassembled
slender strand. Each jewel
a threaded breath   away
from the next.

WHEN I WAS LITTLE

Life made sense
below ground,
when I had no eyes.
I was an earthworm.
Dug tunnels,
ate dead leaves and roots,
healed parts of me
that were lost.
That was when
I could breathe
through my skin.

REAL ESTATE

The house is on sale, the house where I grew up.
"Sleek, sophisticated split-level, three bedrooms."
(There were five when I lived here!)
I walk from room to room, missing everything that isn't there.
Notice the entry floor and family room walls—all re-faced
with a glossy black marble veneer. Gone, the slate floor, and
the one-of-a kind tile mosaic mural. How I loved that mural!
The kitchen, once published in Home magazine—remodeled
in stainless steel and polished granite.
The once-chic pink appliances and center island,
where my family of eight had dinner every night. Gone.
The playroom, where I spent hours playing board games—
Monopoly, Clue, Mousetrap. Now, a state-of-the-art gym.
My parents' bedroom upstairs, so big my mother would set up
a long folding table where my twin brothers and I helped her
to wrap Christmas presents; now so much smaller than I remembered.
Downstairs, where four bedrooms were, now only two.
My bedroom, painted a cave gray. No trace of pink.
But, curiously still hanging from the popcorn ceiling,
the white ball-shaped chandelier. Something of mine still in place.
The real estate agent sees me crying, shoos me out the door.
Later, when I visit my mother,
I tell her our home is just as she remembered it.

IMMERSION

Sometime after midnight,
after long hours leaning
over a low workbench,
my back aching,
I draw a hot bath,
soak under frothy mounds
of soap bubbles that dissolve
like snowflakes on the tongue
Slowly I sink, only my face
above the bath water.
Eyes closed, thoughts float wildly
like loose balloons—
too unwieldy to hold on to.

Sinking deeper,
   I am four again,
   a squirrely little girl
   submerged in the odd-shaped tub
   of my childhood. There,
   behind the wire safety glass,
   my loneliness drifts
   below the foamy surface.
   Under water, I baffle
   the sounds of the house -
   drown out creaking doors
   and rowdy brothers.

I feel the water cradle my body,
slip back into my ripened skin,
hear only my unshaken breathing
and my little girl echo
                rousing me
                        awake.

SAYING GOODBYE

My brother has just flown in from out-of-town work.
He is always busy. Always has something more important to do.
Direct from the airport, he has arrived at the hospital too late.
Unconscious on morphine, my 92-year-old mother
has decided it's time to 'fold her tent."
I've been there all week with another brother, sitting bedside.
I call the rest of our family, tell them mom is dying.
As I say the words, the just-arrived brother—whose travel bag
fills the one chair in the room—glares at me,
waves me away, as if I am one of his employees.
I rush out the door, grieving another loss.

DUSK

The sun,
a magnificent
orange-red orb
dissolves
in smoky haze,
lowers
into the horizon,
disappears.
The heavy ache
of darkness
descends.
Somewhere
the unseen sun
is rising.

AFTER

With your last breath your lips parted,
as if you fell asleep mid-sentence.
Your mouth, a hungry bird, agape.

I cupped your face, drew your lips
to my ear like a conch shell;
heard the hush of your ebbing ocean.

Held your hand, felt your chill.
Saw your tangled fingers uncurl,
your red hair return,
your back upright.

VANISHING POINT

It is not miles ahead of you
where the road narrows.
It is not a mountaintop
covered by low clouds.
Nor, the columns of
trees that grow
smaller farther
down the
street.

It is
a gam
of whales
swimming
just below the
shimmering surface
of the ocean, and you are whale,
and you are water. It is that cloudless
blue sky when birds disappear into the deep
brightness, and you are bird, and you are light.

Melissa is the youngest of six children, and the only girl. She is also an award-winning stained glass and mosaic artist, whose work has been exhibited in galleries and museums. Her current art project is commissioned by the Conejo Valley Public Art Project: a 5 ft., 6 in. cottontail rabbit sculpture completely covered with stained glass mosaic tile. Melissa resides in Simi Valley with her beloved Golden Retriever, Molly.

www.ingramcontent.com/pod-product-compliance
Lightning Source LLC
LaVergne TN
LVHW040118080426
835507LV00041B/1719